PAUL H. DUNN

SUCCESS IS...

Bookcraft • Salt Lake City, Utah

Library of Congress Catalog Card Number: 82-72884
ISBN O-88494-481-6

First Printing, 1983

Lithographed in the United States of America
PUBLISHERS PRESS
Salt Lake City, Utah

Contents

Preface

Often when young adults are asked to define success they commonly respond with answers such as financial security, a home, job status, fame, or some educational accomplishment. These are wonderful and important goals, and they are vital in one's growth and progress. Because of their importance, the world abounds with formulas and instructions on how to achieve success and accomplish goals. But there appears to be a greater and deeper dimension when these accomplishments are measured against heavenly criteria such as "For what is a man profited, if he shall gain the whole world, and lose his own soul?" (Matthew 16:26.)

When more mature persons are asked to define success, such responses as to better know the Savior, to have a closer relationship with one's family, or to gain a better under-standing of self are often given.

Society is so ordered that we all work very hard on achievement, on getting things done and on gaining material things—things. Things are the antithesis of people; and that's the choice we so often face—people or things, relationships or accomplishments.

Success Is... is about people and relationships and how to better understand both.

As always, I am grateful to several for their encourage-ment and assistance. Richard M. Eyre, a long-time friend and associate, has again responded with his usual keen insight and ideas. Sharene Hansen, my able secretary, has read and typed the manuscript. My daughters have again assisted me in keeping the balance. A special word of appreciation goes to my wife, Jeanne, for her constant support and motivation.

Chapter 1

Seven Short Stories

(For Perspective and Reference Points)

The Easy Interview or the Hard One

A Church member once related to me a very interesting discussion she had experienced with her bishop. They knew each other well and as they sat together for a temple recommend interview the bishop found opportunity to teach a principle. He said, "Do you want the easy interview or the difficult one?"

The member, not knowing what to expect, said, "Let's try the easy one first." The bishop then proceeded with the standard interview, reviewing the commandments and the member's general worthiness.

As they concluded, the member's curiosity got the best of her and she asked what the "hard interview" consisted of.

The bishop said, "I'll tell you what the questions are but rather than trying to answer them now why don't you think about them between now and our next interview." Then he outlined a list of questions that included:

When did you last help your neighbor?

When did you last do so anonymously?

When did you last help your enemy?

Which Christlike qualities have you added to your character in the past year?

When was the last time you engaged in earnest, private prayer for fifteen consecutive minutes or more?

In what specific ways have you improved your relationship with your spouse during the last year?

What are the most memorable one-on-one experiences you've had with each of your children recently?

Whom have you forgiven lately?

How often is the priesthood used in your home?

Do you hold any grudges?

Whom do you think you are better than?

How do you prepare for worship in sacrament meeting each Sunday?

What charitable acts have you done during the past month for people less fortunate than yourself?

As my friend left the bishop's office, he had a parting comment for her: "Remember that the rich young ruler who met Christ passed the easy interview." (See Mark 10:17-22.)

The Two Home Teaching Stops

A priesthood holder once described to me the two families that he had home taught for several years:

"I only had the two families, and they were very different from each other. One prosperous, one poor; one on the right side of Main Street, the other just across on the 'wrong' side; one widely known and respected, the other quiet and unknown.

"At first I felt a little intimidated to go to the prosperous family's home. The father was in the stake presidency and was a leading officer in a big company. It was hard to schedule visits because he traveled often and they seemed to have guests whenever they were at home. The longer I was their home teacher, the more I realized that this family (we'll call them Family A) needed help *more* than Family B.

"I always liked to go to Family B's house. At first I thought it was just because they were less threatening to me and, therefore, more comfortable. There was never the kind of tension and impatience in the air that I found at Family A's home. I started going to B first each month because the sweet, peaceful spirit I always found there made me feel more capable of handling the tension of A.

"As months passed and the patterns of B's serenity and peace and A's stress and tension remained consistent, I began to ask myself why. Certainly there is nothing inherently wrong with being busy and heavily involved and successful, and for that matter, Family B was busy and involved too, just in less visible and prominent ways.

"I gradually realized that the answer to my question lay with the fathers. Father A was a good man in many ways but he gave priority to his job and his church work ahead of his family. I'm sure he wouldn't have admitted this. In fact, I'm sure he didn't realize it. But as I knew him longer, the fact became clear. He simply didn't have time or take time to do much with his wife and children. They respected him but they didn't know him very well.

4

"Father B, on the other hand, always had time, always took time. There was a trust level, a sense of security and identity that resulted. Father B simply gave priority to his family above all else.

"I'm sure the relative merits of the two men's lives could be debated extensively, but the one clear irrefutable thing in my mind is the difference in the feeling of those two homes. One I always wanted to stay and bask in. The other I always felt at least slightly anxious to escape from."

The Dream of the White Room

I was told of a penetrating and memorable dream that a woman had. The dream started with her death and she saw her own spirit dressed in a simple white frock, standing in a stark, bare white room. She had no friends around her, no possessions, no facades or impressions to hide behind. She had no titles, no diplomas, no credentials. She was just herself. She had only what was within herself. She was only who she was.

And she was about to meet God.

The Fireside

A friend of mine mentioned a speech he had recently given to a group of select, wonderful young people in their late teens, all with the promise and challenge of missions, marriage, and life in front of them.

5

He asked them to write down their three most important goals for the year ahead. There were many good and worthwhile objectives listed—grades in school, qualification for scholarships, reading and memorizing preparation for missions, completion of various projects, savings from summer jobs, perfect attendance at church meetings, the reading of books of scripture, the achievement of music or sports goals, and so on.

As he analyzed their responses, something became very clear and very disturbing. All of their statements were in *external* terms, things they wanted to accomplish, to do, to bring about, to realize. None were stated internally, in terms of what they wanted to become inside, what specific qualities they wished to gain, what character traits, what relationships with God and with others they hoped to develop.

We wondered (and worried) whether the Lord would not be more concerned with (and pleased with) *internal* objectives than external ones.

The Funeral

I was speaking at the funeral of a truly wonderful man, yet a man that the world would have called common, undistinguished. As I sat in my place on the stand waiting for my turn to speak, I felt an urgency to somehow convey the inner greatness of this man, to communicate that he had accomplished the truly important things of raising a solid family, serving his fellowmen in simple, basic ways, and developing within himself the Christlike qualities of peace and tolerance and a pure heart.

I remembered a conversation with him a week before he died. "I'm worried about the hereafter," he had said. "I've done so little to qualify myself to return to the Lord." I had known less worthy, less pure men who had approached death more confidently, men who held up their more visible accomplishments and offices and recognitions as assurances of their own salvation.

I thought of the scriptural statement, "He that findeth his life shall lose it: and he that loseth his life for my sake shall find it." (Matthew 10:39.) I wondered, as I sat there on the stand, if another similar statement might also be true. "He who proudly thinks he has earned salvation probably has not, while he who humbly worries that he has not probably has."

Olga and the Big Rock

Long ago in the old country there lived a woman called Olga. She was known throughout her village for her thoughtfulness and compassion. Whenever someone was sick, or moved to a new home, or had more work than they could manage, Olga was there to help. No one ever had to ask her. She seemed to know instinctively where help was needed, even when the need was not obvious.

One of Olga's friends (indeed, all of the people in the village were her friends) was another woman of similar age named Helga. Helga was the town gossip. She knew everything about everyone, and tried to be sure everybody knew everything about everyone. Helga was also very self-righteous, and she was meticulously careful never to violate any of the laws of her religion and her society. She was so busy with her gossip and her self-righteousness that she had no time for anything else, certainly not for giving help to people who hadn't even asked.

7

One day Olga committed a sin. She broke one of the rules. It happened in a moment of weakness. She didn't try to hide what she had done, and she felt extremely guilty about it.

The next day Helga showed up at her door. "The whole town knows about your sin, Olga, you poor dear," she said, "and I am here to help you, to give you some advice. Go to the old sage who lives on the mountaintop. Only he can tell you how to repent. In fact, I will go along with you to help you tell him what you have done."

Olga had never met the old sage before, but she had heard that he was very wise and very good. After hiking all morning they reached his mountaintop, and Olga, with a measure of overly anxious help from Helga, told him of the sin.

The old sage, who knew a great deal about both women, told Olga he would teach her of repentance. He said, "Behind my house is a very large stone. Go and get it. Bring it to me."

While Olga struggled with the stone, the old sage's eyes moved to Helga. "Take this large cloth bag," he said, "and go into the garden and fill it as full as you can carry with small stones, none bigger than a penny. Then bring it here to me." After some complaining and protests of "It's her that needs your advice, not me," Helga finally went out to do as he asked.

They struggled back into the house about the same time, Olga bent double under her big stone, Helga struggling and cursing as she dragged the full bag.

"Now," said the sage, "I will teach you of repentance. Olga, take that large stone and return it . . . precisely to where you got it. Helga, take each of those small pebbles and return them to their original places. Do not mix them up or misplace them. The pebbles of omission will be, for you, a much greater burden than Olga's stone of commission."

The Definer

A man lived on the earth once, many centuries ago, who led no armies, made no fortunes, ran for no political office, appeared on no society pages, cultivated no "influential connections," entered into no "mutually beneficial compromises," wrote no books, obtained no degrees or diplomas, assumed no titles, set no fashion trends, placed no plaques on his wall, lived in no great house, was an officer in no business, never became a part of society's mainstream—in short, who achieved none of the usual or traditional hallmarks of success.

He did, however, love and serve all those he met, obey God totally, follow every impulse from the Spirit, keep his second estate, make his calling and election sure, set a perfect example, and save all of mankind.

The Savior redefined success and exposed the world's definition for what it has always been and will always be—a deception.

9

Chapter 2

Success:
The World's
Definition

One of our country's astronauts, one of the handful of human beings who have walked on the surface of the moon, sat back in his chair and considered whether he wanted to answer the question he had just been asked.

He was in a small group, with close acquaintances, so he decided to respond. The question was a basic one: "What did it feel like to stand on the moon and watch the earth rise?"

"I don't talk about that very often," he said, "partly because it's hard to express what I felt and partly because the things I felt were so deep and so personal that I'm careful who I say them to."

Then he talked about how beautiful the earth looked as it rose on the moon's horizon—and how small and how fragile. He said there was something about seeing the whole orb of earth, tiny in the immensity of space, that gave him a perspective he had never felt before. He thought of all the humanity down on that globe, under that cloud cover—planning business deals, accumulating possessions, competing with each other, looking for something they call success—and he realized, with a clarity he'd never known before, how little any of that means and what a short time any of it lasts.

We'll return to the astronaut's observations later. Let's leave him on the moon for now and go down onto the surface of the shining globe he sees under that fleecy cloud cover for a closer look at the world and at how it defines the word *success*.

When you put it to people in the form of a question, *success* turns out to be more difficult to define than one might expect. You get answers that range from being able to have anything you want to finding inner peace. Virtually everyone "wants to suceed." Yet when asked just what the word really means to them, the usual answers are either broad visions of wealth and fame or general platitudes about fulfillment and serenity. Whether people admit it or not, material possessions most often become their yardstick of success, largely because money is the simplest scorecard, the easiest evaluation.

Success books or self-help books line the walls of most bookstores. Browsing through them provides some interesting observations. They can be divided into two broad categories: *money* success books and *alternative-to-money* or anti-money success books. The first group, of course, devotes itself to all the ways of making more money and starts with the basic assumption that *everyone* wants and needs and sets as a top *priority* more money. The second group stakes its claim on both *sides* of money, either telling us how to get the things that *breed* money (power, recognition, influence) *or* how to shake the need for more money altogether and find instead the more ethereal pleasures of inner serenity and self-actualization.

There is one great, sprawling, semiconscious assumption that weaves itself like a common thread through the whole shelf of "success" books. It is the assumption that whatever the books advocate or give formulas for (be it wealth, power, serenity, or whatever), these things provide one with or lead one to happiness.

Happiness is the real objective of all the books. Sometimes that fact is stated; more often it is assumed. It is assumed that more money (or more power or more positive mental attitude or whatever the book advocates) yields more happiness.

That assumption is the problem.

Huge fields of study, areas of expertise, and countless lives have been built on and around false assumptions of what produces happiness.

Some might call it a magnificent simplification for Satan. He doesn't have to teach us to lie or cheat, to exploit or take advantage of, to commit adultery or forsake families.

He just assists us with various wrong definitions of happiness and success, and we do all those other things automatically.

By getting us to accept the wrong definition of happiness and, therefore, to give priority to the wrong goals, Satan puts us in a no-win situation. If we put the bulk of our energy and time into the pursuit of wealth, or recognition, or position, or status, one of two things will happen.

1. We will fail to reach those goals and will feel the dejection and insecurity that makes us vulnerable to Satan's arsenal of self-pity, depression, loss of self-esteem, loss of faith.

2. We will succeed in reaching those goals, perhaps losing ourselves and our families in the process, and become susceptible to Satan's other approach of pride, vanity, self-righteousness, and self-centeredness.

Take a momentary break now from this book. Put your bookmark in at this page, close the book, and put it on the shelf. Then open the Book of Mormon and read Jacob's denunciation of the incorrect priorities and erroneous success definitions of the Nephites. (See Jacob 2:12-21.)

Let's look a little more personally at what the wrong definitions of success and happiness can cause in individual lives.

Robert B. defined success essentially as achievement, and he adopted the criteria that seemed accepted by his community and his society. Through the means of education, corporate politics, very hard work, and a few deals and

14

compromises, he climbed the business ladder until he had the title, the large office, the many employees that testified of his success. It was only after he had them all that he realized that, because of the way he pursued them, they had cost him his health and his honor, his family and his freedom, his faith and his feelings.

Lawrence M. defined success in an almost opposite direction. Freedom from responsibility was what he wanted. Not a busy office on Wall Street, but an unbusy condominium in Hawaii. Early retirement and a chance to do only the things one really wants to do, only the things of ease and pleasure. When he reached his objective, what he found was the quiet hell of boredom and the absence of challenge.

William C. wanted fame. To his mind, wealth and comfort and even power meant little unless others recognized him for them. What he wanted was a nod of deference from passers-by on the street, embarrassed autograph requests from strangers, a name frequently in print, and a face often in view. When it all came, he found an ironic loneliness, a situation where he was constantly surrounded by people who knew of him but who didn't really know him. He himself began to wonder if he knew anyone at all.

15

Collin W. had none of the above problems. He had decided (and told others frequently) that he wanted nothing of position, wealth, or fame, that they all corrupted and that none were for him. He had arrived at this decision after trying and failing at them all. Now that he had decided that they were all evil, he realized that he had never wanted them very badly anyway, and he had an easy and convenient excuse for a life of mediocrity.

The first three individuals felt that position, wealth, and recognition were good. The fourth fellow decided they were bad.

All four are wrong. These things are not good or bad. They do not, in themselves, equate to happiness or to sadness.

They are things of the world. And things of the world may add to happiness or subtract from happiness, may bring about good or evil, may serve others or rob others, depending on the true nature of him who has them.

President Joseph F. Smith said, "It is true that such *secondary* greatness [things of the world] may be added... but when [it] is not added to that which is fundamental, it is merely an empty honor." (*Gospel Doctrine*, page 285.)

16

The message of all four stories is, "Beware of what you want, for you might get it."

But the even deeper message is, "Whatever else you seek, seek first what the Lord defines as success." We will look at his definition in the next chapter.

But first let's be brutally honest for a moment and look at what definitions of success *we* accept. Let's list some of the world's definitions and see which, if any, fit us as well.

The world (or parts of it) measures success by:

1. Wealth and material.
2. Self-gratification.
3. Education, position, and "importance."

4. Freedom from responsibility.
5. Appearances.
6. Conquest (beating others).
7. Recognition and influence.
8. Amorality and "freedom" from restrictions.

Which of those definitions does our Church culture pay homage to? Notice that we are talking about our Church *culture*, not the Church. The Church itself, being God's church, accepts no false definitions of success. But the culture that has grown up *around* the Church, what does *it* accept? What definitions does it honor?

Look again at the list. It's a little disturbing to realize that we generally pay homage to at least half the list. The even numbers are not usually a problem for us; our culture as well as our religion condemns self-gratification, failure to accept responsibility, conquest of others, and amorality.

But what about the other four? What about the odd numbers? Is it possible that we measure our own success a little too much by these four yardsticks of the world rather than by God's definition? And do we judge the worth and success of others by looking at these deceptive criteria? Let's look at some illustrations which are not only true but also recurringly true.

1. A slightly eccentric individual moved into a ward and was received by some members with attitudes that ranged from coolness to disdain. In future weeks, as they discovered his new Mercedes and his address in the best part of town, these same members quickly developed the qualities of friendliness and warmth.

2. I was speaking to a Church member from Washington, D.C., who was telling me what a feather it is in the Church's cap to have so many members so highly placed in the President's administration. The longer he talked, the more I realized that it was the *positions* he judged the men by and not what they did with those positions or how they handled the heavy responsibilities given to them.

3. A man I know recently took a new, higher-paying job in a field he does not like with a company that will require far more travel than will be good for his family. The higher salary of the new job allowed him and his family to move onto the East Bench and park their two new cars in a wider driveway.

18

4. In a ward that was recently split, a young father was called to be the new bishop. The man had always been a good family man, helping his wife with their three small children and including her in all of his plans and thoughts. As the bishop, he found himself the center of attention. People asked him more questions, listened more carefully to what he said. He began to stay even longer at the church than was necessary. He had his family picked up for church by a friend rather than going home for them. He scheduled meetings three of five week nights at the church. He told his wife their relationship would just have to change while he was serving as bishop.

Now, is there anything wrong with a nice home or car, with a position of honor or importance, with a church calling of responsibility? No. What is wrong is measuring our success by any of these, or judging the success or worth of others by them.

What we do with any of these things is far more relevant to success than the fact that we have gained them or that they have been given to us.

Because we have the perspective of the gospel, when we take the time to think about the matter we usually know what true success is and what it isn't. But we live in the world. And the world, to a large extent, values the wrong things. The danger is that people achieve what they truly want. Thus the great need to examine ourselves; because if we accept (even subconsciously) the world's definition of success, we will inevitably pursue it at the expense of *real* and *inner* success.

Examining ourselves. That is the heart of this book's challenge. If we do examine, if we do think, if we do *use* the truths and perspectives the gospel gives us, then we will know and we will see. We will look more closely at the Joneses before we try to keep up materially with them. We will ask ourselves before becoming workaholics whether we work to live or live to work. We will realize that we don't want the fashions and whims of men to define success for us.

Let me tell some stories at this point, true stories of people within the Church who have attempted to come up with a gospel-based definition of success for their own individual lives. Reflect for a moment on what you think of each and on which one is most similar to your own ideas.

1. I think first of a man, sitting in his office, president of a large corporation, explaining that he felt that the way to serve the Lord was to build a certain recognition level and solid financial independence so that he could retire and then

19

give full-time service to the Church from a position of influence and wide-reaching impact.

2. Next I think of a younger man, sitting in my office,
explaining that his desire to serve the Lord was so strong
that he had decided to shelve his hard-earned law degree
and go into full-time seminary teaching so that he would not
have to have a division in his life between what he did for a
living and what he did for the Lord.

3. A more common experience than either of the above
is the Church member who takes the simple and quite
wonderful view that it doesn't matter so much what one
does for a living. Rather, it matters what example is set,
what contributions and kindnesses are made along the way,
and what goes on inside one's heart.

4. An acquaintance of mine has a success model that is
based almost entirely on one word, *obedience.* He simply feels
that if he does everything the Lord says in his commandments, everything the Lord asks in his callings, he will be
rewarded and blessed and his life will be successful in the
Lord's eyes.

5. I know another individual who is, as we all should
be, looking forward to the Lord's second coming. He has a
personal success model that is built around his anticipation of
that event. He feels that the two things necessary in preparation for the event are the preservation of America and the
strengthening of the Church. Thus he devotes his efforts to
those two noble goals.

6. A young lady once told me that she viewed her patri-

archal blessing as personal scripture, that she felt it was a God-given blueprint for what her life should contain and for what her own personal definition of success should be. She had memorized the blessing and sought at every turn to make her life conform to it.

7. A very gifted young missionary offered his idea of what gospel-oriented success actually is. He said he felt the answer was contained in the phrase "... unto whom much is given much is required." (D&C 82:3.) He said that he viewed his gifts and his blessings as tools given to him by God in the expectation that he would use those tools to do God's work and serve his children.

8. A brother possessing a strong and deep testimony once indicated to me that in choosing his major in college he had asked himself the question, "What contribution can I make that is most unique?" He said that the question not only made him look at his individual gifts but also made him realize that many well-intentioned people of all persuasions are capable of making contributions in medicine, in engineering, in law, and so on, and that his knowledge of the restored gospel and the eternal family gave him the opportunity to contribute things that few others could. He became a marriage counselor and part-time institute teacher.

21

9. A very family-oriented member whom I respect highly uses a model of success that he calls the "kingdom model." His view is that God's family is essentially a kingdom, of which we all are part. He believes that the head of that great kingdom, namely God, has put us here to begin our own kingdoms—to promulgate them, to institutionalize them, to make them eternal. These kingdoms become part of God's kingdom (envelopes within envelopes) and thus

bring us a portion of his glory while at the same time adding to his glory.

In my view, all of these "Mormon definitions of success" have some good aspects. All of them also have some voids, some incompleteness. And most of them are tailored for the particular perspective of a single individual. In the next chapter, I would like to pose five questions that I believe, taken together, give a more complete impression of how God measures and defines success.

But before we move to the next chapter and to the Lord's five measurements, let's look, for contrast, at five questions the world asks, five measurements by which the world evaluates success. You will know, as you read them, that they are the wrong questions and the wrong measurements, but they will set the stage for the five right questions that begin the next chapter. When you have read both sets of five, you will realize that the wrong set is a clever counterfeit of the right set.

The world asks:

What brings pleasure?

What gives us glory (recognition, fame)?

What can we consume (use up)?

What can we do to others (to get gain for ourselves)?

How can we keep the status quo and fit into it (without rocking the boat, without risking anything)?

Chapter 3

Success: God's Definition

What brings joy?

What gives glory to God?

What can we retain (take with us eternally)?

What can we do to ourselves and our families (within ourselves and *within* our families)?

How can we change and progress?

What may at first look like subtle or small differences between the world's list and the Lord's list are, in fact, 180-degree differences—opposites. Lives that are governed by the world's list end in dismay and stagnancy. God's list brings about the energies and elevations of eternity. Take a moment. Look closely at the two lists. Evaluate the differences. Ask yourself honestly which list you live by.

But before we probe the true definitions of success further, let's return to the astronaut we mentioned in the previous chapter, standing on the surface of the moon, and let's look this time at the more positive aspects of his observations.

He said that after he had contemplated the unimportance of the schemes and ambitions of men, he looked out again at the beautiful orb of earth, and he longed for home. He missed his family with an acuteness never felt while being on the same planet with them. From the moon he saw the earth as a creation, and he knew that the most important part of the creation was the family of the Creator. He knew at that moment that the things that mattered were the will of that Creator and the children of that Creator.

24

What a perspective he had! How wonderful if all mankind could see the earth from that perspective, could look down at it from above and realize its beauty, its purpose, its priorities, and the joy it has to offer us!

As I ponder this idea, I realize that we, at one time, had this perspective. From our premortal existence, we looked down on the earth, made for us by God; and as we realized that we could go down and experience mortality on it, we "shouted for joy." (See Job 38:4-7.)

We knew—we *must* have known—from that perspective, what constituted real success. We knew what mattered was how much real joy we found, how much glory we gave our Father, how much we changed and improved our own inner selves and the kingdom of our families.

The key is to retain (or regain) that perspective, and to strive to succeed in terms of God's definition of the word.

So let's look deeper at the gospel's measurements of success—at the five questions that opened this chapter.

What Brings Joy?

Scripture tells us that Adam made the choice of mortality so that man might have joy. (See 2 Nephi 2:25.) What is it about mortality, with all of its disappointments and pain, that brings joy? What is it that is different here that increases our capacity for joy? What do we have here that we did not have there? Let's make a list:

25

1. Physical bodies and a physical earth.

2. Self-destiny, the chance to turn agency into freedom.

3. Personal relationships that involve opposition and interdependency and other elements that likely were not possible before.

4. The opportunity to assume God's role of parent— whereas we had always before been only children.

5. The chance to walk by faith and to gain spiritual knowledge of our own through the Spirit.

6. Personal needs and the opportunity to meet the personal needs of others and render service as surrogates of the Savior himself.

Each of these things represents a change from the premortal existence. Does each represent a chance for joy?

In his book *The Discovery of Joy*,[1] Richard Eyre has defined four separate levels of joy that mortality offers to mankind and that God has sent us here to gain. The levels match up with our list.

Level 1. *The joy of body, earth, and agency,* of mortality's three free gifts. As we use and develop each of the three, the first level of joy is obtained.

26

Level 2. *The joy of achievement and relationships.* As we devote our agency to the achievement of worthwhile goals and the development of eternal relationships (particularly those within a family), we gain the second level of joy which also enhances and burnishes joy.

Level 3. *The joy of knowledge.* As we gain faith and nurture it into knowledge, we gain a third level of joy. With it, we realize that the joys of earth and agency, the joys of relationships and achievements, can be permanent, can last forever and fit into the Lord's eternal plan.

Level 4. *The joy of service and of a personal relationship with the Lord.* As we serve the Lord and come to know him, we feel his love and his acceptance and satisfaction of our lives and

[1]Bookcraft, 1974.

through it we gain a fourth level of joy that protects and preserves Level 1, Level 2, and Level 3 eternally.

Without question, one of God's measurements of success is joy. We can make it our measurement as well. We can consciously seek and obtain each of the four levels of joy. And we can do so with the assurance that we are pleasing God and fulfilling our mortal purpose as we do so.

What Gives Glory to God?

A former member of the First Presidency of the Church, late in his life in a general conference where he was too weak to make an address, was called on to offer the benediction. In his prayer was deep insight. One of his phrases was, "Oh, Lord, bless us all with an understanding of our own unimportance."

This great old patriarch, who had lived so long and accomplished so much, was acknowledging that all is God's, that we are mere stewards, that our importance lies in the fact that we are his children.

Indeed, just as it is his work and glory to bring about our eternal life, our work should simply be his glory.

Those who understand the great principle of stewardship realize that the only meaningful success of man is God's success. That we succeed only as we work for his success. True understanding of *stewardship* changes the definition of many other words. *Sacrifice* simply becomes the giving up of something *for* something better. *Service* simply means doing the work of our master, who is not always physically here to do it himself. And *success* simply means loving God and pleasing him and giving glory to him.

Indeed, we must grasp the basic fact that even the most fantastic of worldly successes or wealth or positions become absolutely pale and meaningless when compared with the promises of the temple and with a small place in the Lord's kingdom.

People who live their lives on various levels are motivated by different things.

—Some want only to get by, to survive.

—Some want to achieve for the recognition of others.

—Some honestly seek to please themselves, to meet their own standards.

—Some seek to glorify God and magnify their stewardships.

It is the fourth category that succeeds.

Real success is often known only to the individual and to the Lord. False success is frequently known to many.

Simply to become conscious of the goal of glorifying God can make an enormous difference in an individual life. If we try to make our thoughts glorify God we will eventually think as he thinks. If we attend church with the goal of glorifying God we will find new and deep meaning in the songs we sing, the lessons we hear, the sacrament we partake of. If we glorify God in how we treat our families we will often know instinctively how to handle problems and we will ultimately fold the small kingdom of our eternal families into his ultimate kingdom.

A friend once told me that as a young boy he never once left his home without hearing these words from his mother, "Son, remember who you are." The meaning of the phrase was deeply important: Remember your name, remember that you represent your parents, remember that you have a legacy and a standard to uphold.

A way to true success (by the Lord's definition) is to remember who we are with regard to him. We are his children. We are his subjects. We owe him all. Our whole purpose and objective should thus be to give him glory, through all we think and do and through our constant worship of him.

29

What Can We Retain (Take With Us Eternally)?

A U.S. senator decided not to seek reelection. He said that he could not see true purpose in what he was doing, that he felt there must be more important priorities in life that he had neglected, that he needed to "drop out" and look within himself and strive to find life's purpose.

About the same time, there was a particular teenager who, like so many of his peers, became disoriented in life.

He saw hypocrisy all around him. He found his life to be shallow and meaningless. Nothing really seemed important. He had no purpose. So he dropped out, left school and family, looked everywhere, and tried everything (including drugs) to find something that he desperately needed but could not recognize.

In another part of the world, also at about the same time, a housewife threw up her hands one day and walked out on her family, never to return. She felt used, she said, and abused. She was a doormat. Her husband and children walked on her. She knew that there must be something more to life. So she dropped out and undertook her own search for priorities, for purpose, for something "important" in life to cling to, to identify with, to be fulfilled by.

30

Three different people, in three different places and three sets of different circumstances, but all reacting the same, all dropping out, and all lacking the same essential thing: a sense of purpose and priorities.

True success is knowing what really matters. It is knowing what has lasting value. It is pursuing the things that endure.

Purpose is joy. And joy is purpose. If the housewife had understood the plan of salvation she would have found meaning in every small thing she did for her family. If the teenager had possessed the goals and purpose of the gospel's framework, he would have better understood the people and circumstances around him and found meaning in his individual life. If the senator had known the purpose of life, he would have found purpose in his public service.

Things of the world, while they may provide some pleasure and some temporary sense of satisfaction, do not endure and therefore cannot be included in any long-term definition of success.

Some "things of the world" may contribute to our eternal success, but they will do so indirectly, according to what we learn in gaining them and how we use them in the help and service of others.

The scriptures tell us of circumstances in which the things of the world have become slippery, that they can disappear like quicksilver, that if they are valued too highly, we may lose ourselves when we lose them. (See Helaman 13:31-36; Mormon 1:17-19.) And, of course, they are not ours anyway, but God's. As mere stewards, how foolish we are if we begin to think of God's things as ours, if we begin to lust after things that cannot belong to us, at least not now!

31

I spoke not long ago to a man who had once held high public office. His name had been recognized by the public, and his face as well. He had passed bills and made important speeches. He told me that no one remembered much of what he had done anymore. He told me he was even forgetting a lot of it himself. I said, "No one remembers?" He said, "Well, my family does." Then we spent a little time talking about the fact that it was his family that counts. He told me that he wished he had spent more time giving them memories of personal time together and experiences as a family and a little less time giving them memories of himself as an "always too busy" public office holder.

God's definition of success revolves around the eternal. So let's ask ourself the classic question, "What can we take with us?" It's a question often asked, but without the gospel it is never fully or satisfactorily answered. Within the gospel, however, there are clear answers, answers that help us define what real (and eternal) success is. The list is not long, but its implications are so important and so sweet.

1. Our families.
2. Our relationships.
3. Our faith and testimony.
4. Our knowledge.
5. Our character.

Five things. Five things that we can gain here and retain forever.

If we pursue them, our lives will be meaningful. If we give them the right priorities, our day-to-day living will have purpose. If we seek them, our mortal lives will become successful in the immortal sense of the word.

What Can We Do to Ourselves and to Our Families (Within Ourselves and Within Our Families)?

A father once took his son on a hike in the mountains. The father was a high-achieving personality—aggressive and ambitious, perhaps to a fault. But he loved his son and wanted to be a good father.

On this particular day, they started early with the objective of reaching the high mountain meadow before nightfall so they could pitch their tent and make camp for the night.

They struggled on throughout the day, most of their conversation centered on how far they had gone, how much daylight they had left, how far they had to go. The boy became tired and complained. The father told him to be tough and endure. The boy tried. When it became too much for him, his father, acting disappointed, took the boy's pack along with his own, and they struggled on. When the boy wanted to rest, the father pushed him on. When the boy wanted to stop and look at something, the father reminded him that they were losing valuable time.

Sometime later in the day, about midafternoon, the *33* father glanced over at the face of his son, and for the first time really *saw* what was going on. The boy was holding back the tears—not wanting to disappoint his dad, plugging on but not enjoying any part of it. Something about the boy's face caused the father to make the most important discovery of his life—the discovery that there are always *two* kinds of goals that exist together. One is to get to the top of the mountain. And the other is to enjoy the journey, to learn and grow from it, to understand from it, to form relationships during it. He realized that the second goal is always present, whether the first goal is climbing a mountain, or building a business, or filling a church assignment. And he realized that the second goal is almost always more eternally important than the first. It is the journey that counts. It is what is learned and shared and noticed and enjoyed along the journey that matters and that lasts.

The man stopped. He turned to his boy and took him in his arms. He told him he had just realized that it didn't matter a bit if they got to the top that day. He told him that what mattered is that they loved each other and that they were together.

In the days and years that followed, the man remembered that simple experience, and it changed his life.

There are two kinds of goals in everything we do. Two dimensions to every experience. One is the *external* (the climbing of the mountain); the other is the *internal* (the feelings, the understanding, the communication, the things that happen *inside* during the journey).

34   The *internal* is the true measure of success.

The Savior spent thirty years working on his own internal understanding and perfection (and an eternity prior to that). He then spent three years giving it to the external world. And his message, of course, dealt only with the internal, with who we each are and who we each are becoming.

He taught us that if we wish to make the outside clean we must first cleanse the inside. (See Matthew 23:26.)

He cautioned us not to be like the whited sepulchre, a facade of brightness, but decayed and dark within. (See Matthew 23:27.)

He told us not to fear outer things but the destruction of the inner soul. (See Matthew 10:28.)

He warned us of the folly of building on the sand of external things of the world, of trying to serve two masters, and of looking for treasures on earth. (See Matthew 7:24; 6:26; 6:19.)

It is interesting to note that it was Matthew who re-membered and recorded these particular admonitions — Matthew, who had been a man of the world, oriented previously to external definitions of success, Matthew who now followed Christ and had come to realize that only the internal things truly last and truly matter.

If we take an honest and candid look at our personal objectives and goals, many of us will find that they are external in nature. We are trying to earn a certain degree, or make a certain salary, or own a certain home. Even gospel-related goals are often stated and thought of in external terms (read a certain number of pages in scripture, attend a certain percentage of meetings or a certain number of temple sessions).

All of these goals may be good, but we need strong internal goals to go with them. (Becoming more Christlike, developing a stronger testimony, gaining certain character qualities.)

Benjamin Franklin, without the benefit of the restored gospel, nonetheless became a master of internal objectives. He would decide on a quality or character trait that he desired and then concentrate on that quality to make it a part of him. Then he would choose another and pursue it in the same way.

The same kind of internal thinking needs to occur within our families. Again, we too often think externally—what school we want to get our children into, what time we want to spend together on vacation, what lessons we want to cover in family home evenings. Again, these goals are good but are not meaningful without internal goals (full trust for each other, full support for each other, family traditions of service and excellence).

We must learn to ask ourselves more questions that start with who. Who are we becoming within ourselves? Who are we becoming within our families? Whose life is being influenced for good by our life?

The Lord's definition of success is an inner definition. When we stand before him we will have no external props or credentials. We will have only what we are—inside.

How Can We Change and Progress?

Those who seek some kind of guaranteed "sameness" or security often find stagnancy instead.

And there are those of us who use a warped view of the gospel perspective as an excuse for this stagnation. We say, "The things of the world are evil," or, "I don't look for recognition or fame in the eyes of men," or, "I avoid the kind of responsibility that keeps me from my family and my church." But too often what we really mean is, "I'm not really achieving too much or putting forth very much effort, but I'll use the external perspective as an excuse for not accomplishing much in the earthly perspective."

What we forget is that we can be just as wrong on this extreme end of the spectrum as on the other extreme end. It is just as wrong (and just as damning) to ignore the challenges and potential for true achievement and growth within our world as it is to covet and worship them.

Again, it is not the things of the world that are wrong, it is our giving them priority above the things of the Spirit. It is not that we should turn away from the challenges of the world, it is that we should keep them in perspective and meet them for God's glory and use them to do his work.

Remember the parable of the talents. It was the servant who buried his talent who was punished. It was the person who was dormant who had his talent taken away. And the talent was given to the servant who had the most, who had used and multiplied his talents.

37

Of course, we must give priority to the right things in life—strive to climb the right mountain. But I often think that, in many ways, someone who climbs the wrong mountain is still better off than one who stayed forever in the valley below.

We can learn from our mistakes. We can adjust our priorities. If we are "actively engaged" we can constantly reevaluate to see that we are engaged in the right thing. What is truly displeasing to God is our being not engaged fully in anything. It was he who said, "...because thou art lukewarm, and neither cold nor hot, I will spue thee out of my mouth." (Revelation 3:16.)

Theodore Roosevelt said:

In the battle of life, it is not the critic who counts; not the man who points out where the strong man stumbled or where the doer of the deed could have done better.

The credit belongs to the man who is actually *in* the arena, whose face is marred by blood and sweat. Who strives valiantly, who does actually strive to do the deeds, and who falls short again and again because there is not effort without failure. Who knows the great vicissitudes, the great challenges and who, if he succeeds, knows the triumph of high achievement and who, if he fails, at least fails while daring greatly, so that his place shall never be among those cold and timid souls who never knew either victory or defeat.

Indeed, the Lord tells us that we are here to subdue the earth and to engage in *eternal progression.* We view the goal of eternity in opposite terms from most of Christianity. They see eternal rest, we see eternal progress.

38

We are told to "be in the world and not of the world," and we sometimes interpret it as justification for removing ourselves from the world, for dropping out of it and taking little interest in it.

Actually, the best interpretation of the statement is as two separate admonitions: 1. Be in the world. 2. Be not of the world. In other words, participate and be active and achieve within the world, but don't value the world above the Spirit. Use the things of the world to serve God. Seek first his kingdom and then all these things (if desired for a righteous purpose) shall be added unto you.

The Lord wants us all to succeed here in the world. And he wants us to consecrate all we have to him, in realization that it all belongs to him anyway. As we adopt this attitude of stewardship and as we seek first his kingdom, he will bless us with stewardships that both test our loyalty and give us opportunity to share, to serve, to contribute, and to grow.

Our purpose is progress. Our progress is purpose. Both equate to joy and to God's definition of success.

Chapter 4

How to Change

(From One Definition to the Other)

The story is told of two brothers who were sheep thieves. After repeated offenses, it was decided that the only way to curtail their activities was to identify them permanently as thieves by branding them with a hot iron. Accordingly, they were rounded up and branded, right across their foreheads, with an ST for "sheep thief."

One of the brothers could not tolerate the humiliation and, after a short period, left the valley, never to be heard from or seen again.

The other brother, however, decided to repent and to change. He devoted himself to good causes, developed a deep sense of inner integrity, and began to live a life of honor and respect. As the years passed, he became known for his selflessness and service.

He lived out his life in this fashion, and when he died the whole valley came to his funeral. In the eulogy the preacher said, "Many have asked what the letters on his forehead mean. I have asked around and no one can remember their exact origin or what they are intended to stand for. Many of us, however, by the evidence of his life, have concluded that ST simply stands for saint."

Can people really change? Can we change our definition of success and the way we live our lives in response to our definition?

Of course we can. The very foundation of the gospel and the Atonement is the assurance that we can change and improve, can put away the old and put on the new. The central premise of the plan of salvation is renewal and improvement and progress.

Let's assume that we all need to do some changing (a fairly safe assumption). And let's assume that all of us can stand to do a little redefining of our own idea of success... to remove it a little from the world's definition and to move it a little closer to the Lord's.

But let's clarify one thing. Knowing that change is possible and acknowledging that we each need it still does not make it easy. Any change, and particularly a change in how we think, is very difficult indeed.

Change is hard for several reasons. First of all, we have probably been doing what we do and thinking what we think for a very long time. Second, other people don't want us to change. Our change often threatens them, makes them feel insecure. People are a little like crabs. You can put two or more crabs in an uncovered bucket and none will ever climb out because another crab will always pull him back down. People tend to want to hold other people down at their level. People who are changing, progressing, thinking, are often perceived as a threat to the comfort and ease of the status quo.

So change is hard—but possible—and when to the right things for the right reasons, wonderful. And there are tried and proven ways to change.

Before we get into them, however, let's take a little closer look at the kinds of changes we are talking about.

We are talking about changing our thinking, changing our definition of success to more closely match the Lord's definition, and then changing our actions, our thoughts, and our priorities to match our new definition.

Think for a moment of the implications. If we can teach ourselves to look more for joy and less for pleasure, we will find ourselves studying harder, praying harder, working harder on things like gratitude, relationships, inner peace. If we can change our focus from what gives us glory to what gives God glory, we will find ourselves reading our patriarchal blessings more than our press clippings, our scriptures more than our balance sheet. If we can truly learn to think more about the things we can keep forever than about the things we consume, we will be working more for our fellowmen and less for our cars and our investments. If we can think more about what we can change within ourselves and within our families, we will be less likely to worry about what others are doing to us or about what we can do to them. And if we consciously adopt God's goal of spiritual progression and stop trying to fit the world's norms and status quos, we will find that we are more and more in line with the Lord's status quo.

So these are no small changes. They are mind-changing, life-changing, eternity-changing. And they are worth every ounce of effort they require.

They are all changes in the mind, in the spirit, and in the thought pattern, and therefore they require a mental and spiritual approach.

44

These are inner changes that produce outer changes, thought changes that produce action changes.

Some people try to reverse the process. They change what they are doing, in the hope that it will subsequently change what they are thinking. For example, they change what they do with their families, hoping that it will change how they think of and set priorities about their families. To a degree this approach is good, and to a degree it works. But the real changes are the inner ones, and the eight "methods" suggested below seek to change the inner first, with the conviction that the inner will always eventually change the outer. Some of the ideas may seem difficult and even extreme, but bear in mind that what you are attempting to change or adjust is perhaps the thing most resistant to change—yourself.

1. *Prayer for change.* The most inner process is also the most outer, in the sense that we reach out into the universe

and even to God himself to solicit his presence and input to our innermost selves.

By asking the Lord to help us change our thoughts and think more as he would think, we call down the most powerful force of all to help our definitions of success match his. Ask him to help, apply his five success-measuring questions to yourself, then look at life in the perspective of joy, his glory, treasures of heaven, inner change, and progress.

Specific prayer brings about specific blessings. And there is no type of prayer more in harmony with God's purposes for us than a prayer in which we ask for his help in meeting his will for us—his kind of success.

2. *Self-programming.* Just as a computer can be programmed to perform in a particular manner, we can program ourselves to be more aware and thus more responsive to the Lord's definition of success.

Among Church members there exists an interesting and somewhat unpleasant irony. Those with testimonies know full well what life's true priorities should be, yet in the way they live their day-to-day lives many are not noticeably different from those who do not share the gospel's insight. The reason for this is basic and simple. We live so much in the world that it is hard to avoid being influenced by the prevailing ideas and notions about what is successful. In simple terms, it is tough to live in the world without being worldly. We care too much what others think and try too hard to fit the world's norm.

Self-programming is a way of combatting this. It is a way

of reminding ourselves, frequently and powerfully, that we accept the Lord's definition and not the world's. It is that little reminder, that reinforcement of our convictions, that will cause our actions and thoughts to stay consistent with our beliefs.

And that is really all that self-programming is, a regular pattern of reminding ourselves of something. As the previous chapter pointed out, the accurate definition of success includes joy, God's glory, relationships, service, and what we are becoming within ourselves and our families—how we are changing and progressing.

To begin a self-programming pattern, read again the illustrations of these five measurements in chapter 3, then add your own thoughts until each of the five is vivid and clear in your mind. Then pick some predictable and regular daily activity (shaving, brushing your teeth, the moment before morning prayer, etc.) and use that moment *each* day to remind yourself of those five priorities. Remind yourself through recommitment. For example, say to yourself, "I am committed to God's glory. I seek to magnify him in all I do. I try to meet his objectives for me and to have my own objectives fit into his," and so on.

Then, during the day, at moments when you may feel inclined to covet, or to make decisions or time allocations that contradict the true priorities remind yourself again and reinforce your acceptance of the Lord's definition by making the right choice, pursuing the right priority.

3. *Spouse reinforcement.* For those who are married, another way to counter the constant bombardment of the world's

false priorities is spouse-to-spouse. Once a week, on Sundays, probably at an early or late hour when interruption and commotion are minimized, review together the true priorities of life. Commit to each other your intentions to live and plan and make decisions based on accurate and eternal priorities. The love between a husband and wife is what makes this method work. The expectations of one beloved husband or wife can outweigh the expectations of the world. The knowledge that your spouse will measure you by the Lord's definition of success can outweigh the knowledge that the world will measure you by its own definition.

4. *The sacrament.* The partaking of the sacrament carries with it three commitments which we make weekly to our Heavenly Father. One is that we will keep his commandments. One is that we will take upon us the name of Jesus Christ. The third is that we will remember the Savior's life and teachings. All three of these commitments, particularly the middle one, imply that we will accept his priorities and measure our lives by his standards.

47

Therefore, as we partake each week and as we remember his life and his atonement, we can take upon us, once again, his name, and we can take upon us, once again, his definition of success.

5. *Write a "one-year-from-now" description of yourself.* One reason that the world's definitions of success are so easily accepted is that they are so easily measured. Money is easy to measure. All possessions are. And so are certain kinds of recognition, fame, and power. Since they are easy to

measure, they are easy to put in order of priority and to set objectives for.

The eternally important things—things like joy, service, relationships, and personal character—are harder to measure in quantitative terms. We know within ourselves when we are feeling right about these things, but how do we set objectives for specific improvement?

One way is to sit down and write out a description of the person you would like to be one year from now. Attempt to describe the you that you would like to be—in terms of how you think, in terms of what kind of parent you are, how you give and receive joy, the value you put on relationships and service, and so forth.

If you take some time and seriously try to describe what you hope to become, you will be reinforcing and "locking in" the proper priorities of life.

Once you have written the basic document, read it over regularly and add to it as your insights become clearer.

6. *Readjust your time allocation.* Not long ago I asked a group of people in a fireside audience to list their five highest priorities on a slip of paper. It was a gathering of solid Church members, so the results were somewhat predictable. "Families" came in first, then "church," followed by "jobs," "hobbies," "sports," and other interests. Then I asked them to turn the slips of paper over and list the same things again, only this time in order of how much time they had spent working on each. In many cases the lists were reversed—jobs and leisure interests ranking above families

and Church callings. Many of those who responded honestly, particularly fathers, also admitted that they had spent more mental energy on jobs and personal interests than on giving specific input to family matters.

Rousseau said, "Parenting is the one profession where we must learn how to lose time in order to gain it." Our families, particularly our children, need our time and our mental energy. If we "lose" time to them now, we will gain time later—in the sense that they will listen to us and communicate with us longer.

Keep a daily record of how much time you spend in meaningful activity or communication (mental energy being expended) with your family, with work, with hobbies or sports, with Church callings. Total it up at the end of the week.

Then decide how you think the time should be readjusted, and write an "ideal" set of time figures next to the actual ones. You may not have to take time from your job or other activities to spend more with your family. It may be just a question of taking more of the time when there is no meaningful activity or communication and giving it to your top priority.

During the following week, keep a record again and see if you can consciously change your ratio of time so that it meets your goal of where that time and mental energy should be spent.

7. *Ending the day with thoughts of the first priorities.* Some pyschologists tell us that the last things we think about as

we go to sleep at night become the things that we do the next day. Unfortunately, our minds work a little like the squeaky wheel that gets the grease. The pressures and battles of the world weigh on our minds all day and we go to sleep thinking about them instead of about the things of eternal importance.

One way to prevent this is to focus your thoughts on the eternal priorities for a few moments before your bedtime prayer. If you are married, discuss the day together—talk about your children, your relationships, the service you may have rendered. Think about the day ahead and how you can use it to glorify God. Then include in your prayer all that you have thought, and retire feeling recommitted to the right things.

8. *Sunday sessions.*[2] Find time on Sunday (early in the morning is best) to "write your diary in advance," to plan the week ahead based on Heavenly Father's definition of success. Review the "one year away" description of yourself that you have written. Think about your family. Think ahead for opportunities to serve. Think about the quality of your relationships, your personal character, your testimony. Review your patriarchal blessing, your five-year goals, your one-year goals, your one-month goals.[2] Think through next week's calendar and make notes on it to yourself regarding the priorities you will have and the specific things you will concentrate on.

---

[2]For further details on Sunday planning see *Life Planning* by Paul H. Dunn and Richard M. Eyre (Bookcraft, 1979), and *The Secret of the Sabbath* by Richard M. Eyre (Bookcraft, 1982).

A Challenge

I would like to close this rather personal book with a rather personal challenge, one which, if accepted, can change both how you live your life and where you live your eternity.

I challenge you to select an upcoming fast Sunday and to prepare to devote it entirely to your personal redefining of the word *success*. Prepare by rereading this book, making notes of your own thoughts in the margins, and by thinking and praying about your patriarchal blessing and the current directions of your own life.

Arrange your fast Sunday to allow you to have, prior to breaking your fast, two or three private hours. Go to a quiet and secluded place and engage in prayer about the true measurements of mortal success. Ask Heavenly Father to inspire you specifically concerning the things that will make your life a success in his eyes.

Make notes on what you feel. Write down the commitments you feel inspired to make. Write down what you feel should be *your own* life's priorities. Decide which "methods" you will use to change how you think about success. Select them from the list in chapter 4 or from your own mind of ideas.

End your fast with a commitment to Heavenly Father and with a fervent request that the Holy Spirit might assist you in your effort to live your life in harmony with his definition of success.